THROUGH THE EYES
OF THE MASTERS

Polly Wood

Please Return to:-

MASTER RAKOCZI

THROUGH THE EYES OF THE MASTERS

MEDITATIONS AND PORTRAITS

BY

DAVID ANRIAS

AUTHOR OF "ADEPTS OF THE FIVE ELEMENTS,"
"MAN AND THE ZODIAC."

With an Introduction by
THE AUTHOR OF " THE INITIATE," ETC.

With 9 full-page illustrations

LONDON
GEORGE ROUTLEDGE & SONS, LTD.
BROADWAY HOUSE, CARTER LANE, E.C.

First Edition 1932.
Revised Edition 1936.
Third Edition 1947

PRINTED IN GREAT BRITAIN BY
LUND HUMPHRIES
LONDON · BRADFORD

DEDICATED WITH AFFECTION
TO
ROSE AND CYRIL SCOTT
IN
MEMORY OF THE TIME SPENT
AT
RYE DURING 1932

Meditation upon each Adept and his work during this period of transition will help you to realize how even now the difficulties of the future are being considered by the Masters according to their Rays of Evolution. You will then comprehend something of the different methods employed, and the way Humanity is likely to react to their influence in its blind struggles towards the light.

CONTENTS

PORTRAITS

Also known as the Master R or the Comte St. germain

MASTER RAKOCZI. Francis Bacon in a previous incarnation.

MASTER MORYA, a Rajput Prince. Occupied Akbar's body in a previous incarnation. Resides at Shigatse.

MASTER KOOT HOOMI LAL SINGH, of Kashmiri origin. Studied at Oxford in 1850. Pythagoras in one of his previous incarnations. Resides at Shigatse.

MASTER JESUS. Previous incarnation Joshua, son of Nun; also Jesus of Nazareth who was overshadowed by the Christ. Now in a Syrian body. Lives in the Holy Land.

MASTER HILARION. In a previous incarnation St. Paul. Now in a Cretan body. Spends much time in Egypt.

THE VENETIAN MASTER. The painter Paul Veronese in one of his previous incarnations.

MASTER SERAPIS. Greek by birth. Works with the Deva Evolution. Dwelling-place may not be revealed.

THE MAHACHOHAN. Known as the Lord of Civilization. Chief of the Masters. Resides in the Himalayas.

THE LORD MAITREYA. Known to Christians as the Christ, to the Orient as the Bodhi-sattva, to Mohammedans as the Iman Madhi. Appeared in India as Shri Krishna, in Palestine as Christ, in Great Britain as St. Patrick, whose etheric body he now holds. Resides in the Himalayas. His office is that of World Teacher. He presides over the destiny of great religions.

FOREWORD TO THE SECOND EDITION

A NEW and larger portrait has been substituted for the original profile sketch of the Venetian Master. As several people have commented upon the fact that there was no portrait of the Master Rakoczi in the first edition, I have included this sketch as a frontispiece. It depicts Him prior to the death of the Crown Prince Rudolf of Austria[1] and reflects the fashion of that period. This is done for obvious reasons. This Great Adept is chiefly concerned with the destinies of Europe and the two Americas.

Through the window as I write, I can see the long foreshore of Westward Ho!, receiving in ordered sequence the powerful waves of the Atlantic Ocean. From this coast, my forebears, pioneer spirits indeed, were inspired by that mysterious life-force, of which we know so little, to transfer their enthusiasm and vitality to America, the land destined to become the intuitive Sixth Race of the future. This international

[1] See *Adepts of the Five Elements* (Routledge).

FOREWORD TO THE SECOND EDITION

etheric rapport, the strongest tie that exists, was occultly maintained by the Master Rakoczi until the Great War, foreseeing the necessity for that union in the highest element, which withstood "the test of Fire" in a time of world crisis. This tie, despite many past and future difficulties, will continue, for each country needs the other in the future.

Only those who have attained the Fifth initiation and live but for subtle forms of sacrifice on inner planes, beyond the comprehension of the average mind, may invoke the Fire at times of international crisis. There is the psychic record of such a powerful *spiritual* ceremonial, presided over by the Master Rakoczi, close to this coast, which is likely to endure for many years, for three Adepts visited a certain promontory nearby.

David Anrias,
Westward Ho!,
Devon. January 1936.

FOREWORD TO THE THIRD EDITION

THE continued demand for this book has justified a third edition, which, nevertheless, has been delayed owing to paper shortage, brought about by war conditions. This limitation still exists and so it is only possible to stress the most important occult developments that have arisen during the last decade.

My thanks are due to Mr. P. G. Clancy, editor of *American Astrology Magazine*, for permission to reprint excerpts from my article, "The Prevailing Cycle of Mars" This article was written before the last World War, received by him September 7th, 1939, and published in the above magazine January 1940. It is included here as an Appendix, because of frequent references made to it in this and also my other two books, *Adepts of the Five Elements* and *Man and the Zodiac*. The importance of this 35 year cycle cannot be over-estimated regarding occult and mundane matters at a critical period in man's evolution.

FOREWORD TO THE THIRD EDITION

In the foreword of the second edition I stated that in the World War of 1914–18 Master Rakoczi and certain occult forces were associated with this coast line. These forces were strengthened on all planes during the last World War.

There is always a strong tie between an Adept and that country through which he attained the Arhat initiation. As Francis Bacon in a previous life, He was living in the outside world, far in advance of his time, polarized towards a future, which he must have foreseen in flashes of illumination.

Now functioning as an Adept, He returns to this country from time to time, to strengthen certain centres, which are maintained as focii of etheric force, to be drawn upon in time of crisis such as we have lately experienced.

In this way the Adepts function on a plane above personal ambition, unrecognized and unacclaimed; content to be "as nothing in the eyes of men".

North Devon,

August 1946.

PREFACE TO THE THIRD EDITION
NEW METHODS FOR A NEW AGE

THE almost universal conditions of strife and upheaval created by the last World War are but a mundane reflection of the still greater changes and conflicts which occurred on the higher planes within the aura of the earth. Crisis after crisis following in rapid succession, necessitated extraneous aid to overcome the dark forces menacing mankind. The White Lodge required to be increasingly reinforced by Greater and more highly evolved Beings, associated with Sirius and operating through the planet Uranus and the sign Aquarius.

The above statement should not prove too startling an assertion. Hints have been thrown out from time to time that the Changing Age demands new methods of occult development, thereby fulfilling that ancient prophecy: "Behold, I make all things New!"

In this and in my other two books I have already outlined the Aquarian method of occult development.*

* See *Adepts of the Five Elements*, page 57.

PREFACE TO THE THIRD EDITION

I also conveyed that the **Masters** were studying with pupils of the new-race type, the changing conditions through a new occult technique. These pupils are those capable of projecting their conscious and subconscious minds towards the future rather than holding on to the past.*

In *Man and the Zodiac* I conveyed that bodies suitable for those Adepts living in the Hymalayas would not be able to exist amongst those conditions prevailing on the earth at much lower altitudes. The Master Koot Hoomi has asserted in the *Mahatma Letters* (page 285), that an Adept "holds the power of choosing for himself new bodies—whether on this or any other planet—while in possession of his old form, that he generally preserves for purposes of his own".

The general conditions of the present Lunar Cycle (March 1945–March 1980) were anticipated by the Master Koot Hoomi in 1932 and are foretold in pages 36 and 37 of this book. Nevertheless the very

---

* Few pupils will be aware of this relationship in the conscious mind, though all will be experiencing the training in the subconscious. So nothing *spectacular* is likely to materialize for a considerable time. Those pseudo-occultists who claim to be certain Masters or their agents, functioning on this plane and demand financial support in their name now and in the future, should be viewed with distrust.

afflictions of the chart, as a whole, will ultimately bring about a great change of thought: for inner growth is only achieved through experiencing the tension of so-called malefic aspects.

Similarly what He has said regarding the great influx of power to be poured forth at the end of the century (during the Solar Cycle) will come to pass. Some of the greatest leaders and artists the world has ever known will have re-incarnated and will be co-operating with some of the Masters on this plane, under the inspired direction of the Lord Maitreya Himself.

A delineation of this Lunar chart may be published in another book, depending upon the response to what is written about it in this one.

INTRODUCTION

By the Author of *The Initiate in the Dark Cycle*, etc. etc.

I FEEL it a great honour that I should be asked to write an introduction to a book which in many respects is unprecedented in the field of thoughtful literature. During the last fifty or sixty years a portion of the public may vaguely have heard of mysterious sages with alleged extraordinary powers who live somewhere in the Himalayas; those who sought to prove their existence were dismissed either as frauds or Theosophical cranks, or else as persons with highly fertile imaginations. In any event these sages were not regarded as of importance or as in any way taking part in affairs political, artistic, or other non-religious branches of activity concerned with human progress.

That such an assumption is entirely wrong, this book may serve to demonstrate—at any rate to those whose minds are not darkened by a facile and ever-ready scepticism towards all things of which they are ignorant. Yet if it does no more than cause people to reflect, enquire and investigate, it will not have been put forth in vain.

RE-DISCOVERY OF ANCIENT TRUTHS

The present is an age of bewildering contrasts and extremes, in which the most startling scientific discoveries in the Realm of Matter are coincident with equally, or even more startling ones in the Realm of Mind. But whereas the former, as far as we can judge, are new discoveries, the latter are merely re-discoveries of what was known to the ancients. We are, in fact, gradually coming to realize that much which was waved aside by rationalists as mere superstition cannot be disposed of in that high-handed fashion, and that supernormal phenomena, previously supposed to arise through some sporadic intervention on the part of the Deity, were but manifestations of natural forces in the hands of those who knew how to wield them, or of perceptive faculties not as yet operative in the generality of mankind.

Thus what at one time was emotionally termed a miracle, is now more level-headedly categorized as an instance of clairvoyance, clairaudience, hypnotic mesmerism, magnetic or metaphysical healing, as the case may be. Man has discovered that such faculties lie latent in the human organism, and may either be to some extent inherited, or scientifically cultivated under the tuition of a qualified teacher. In that event he is in a position to prove directly through his own perceptions the existence of super-physical planes, of higher states of consciousness, of countless dis-embodied entities and of manifold powers and poten-tialities to which he has heretofore been entirely oblivious. Meanwhile, until he has acquired those faculties himself, he is dependent for his knowledge upon the testimony of others who *have* acquired them, just as he is likewise dependent on the testimony of scientific men with regard to astronomical or other scientific knowledge or phenomena which he has neither the inclination nor the facilities to investi-gate for himself. In a word, occult science is every whit as scientific as material science, and the fact that there are bad, indifferent and even fraudulent occultists can in no measure militate against Truth itself.

INTRODUCTION

Those who are apt to sweep aside Occultism as fanciful nonsense—for I write this introduction less for Theosophists than for the lay reader—will find if they consult the dictionary that *occult* means *existing but not immediately perceptible*. Thus the occultist maintains that in and around us exist planes of being not immediately perceptible, but, as already stated, subject to perception by those who are prepared to develop the necessary faculties. The process of developing these has in India been reduced to an exact science known as Râja Yoga, of which slightly varying forms have been secretly taught in every civilization.[1]

Briefly stated the science of Râja Yoga[2] consists in a number of graduated processes calculated to bring about such an intense and specific concentration of mind that the practitioner, or Yogi, loses all consciousness of his body and becomes for the time-being super-conscious. Expressed in material language, he leaves the physical plane and enters a higher plane of

[1] See E. Shuré, *The Great Initiates*.
[2] See *Râja Yoga*, by Swâmi Vivekanânda. (Various editions.)

consciousness where he undergoes certain ecstatic experiences, and, what is highly important for this argument, brings back the memory of those experiences when he returns to his body. This condition is called *Samâdhi* or super-conscious trance.[1]

To quote Swâmi Vivekanânda :

When the mind has been trained to remain fixed on a certain internal or external location, there comes to it the power, as it were, of flowing in an unbroken current towards that point. . . . When this power has been so much intensified as to be able to reject the external part of perception and remain meditating only on the internal part, the meaning . . . then it acquires knowledge of the finer manifestations of Nature. . . .

and of what occultists call the Higher Planes. This knowledge, however, can be acquired by means other than that of entrancement, which is more suited and appeals more to the Oriental than to the Westerner, who is more active by nature and whose whole organism is differently constituted. Yet by whatever

---

[1] This is not to be confounded with the sub-conscious trance of the spiritistic medium or hypnotic subject ; the latter remembers nothing when the trance is concluded, or if he does remember anything, it is usually too unimportant to be termed Illumination.

scientifically regulated process the finer manifestations are perceived, the practitioner comes to know once and for all that he is immortal, and that our physical plane is but the grossest of all planes of consciousness. If he so desires, he is enabled to contact disembodied entities who once lived on earth, and also the Devas, those hosts of Spiritual Intelligences who are treading a line of evolution different from our own, but who play an important part in carrying out the great scheme of Nature and the government of our Solar System. Further he knows that the doctrine of Reincarnation is a fact, and that the law of sequence and consequence, termed Karma,[1] is also a fact. He knows that he possesses not merely a physical body but other bodies of much rarer matter which envelop and interpenetrate that physical body and also inter-penetrate each other.[2] Finally, if he persists and attains the goal of this age-old science of Yoga, he will reach the Nirvanic plane, the plane of complete, eternal and unconditional Bliss.

[1] As expressed in the Biblical text " As a man sows, so shall he reap ".

[2] These subtler bodies he can see around his fellow-men in the form of auras which vary in size and colour according to the development and character of each individual.

When a man has reached Nirvana[1] or Liberation he is not compelled to retain his physical body or to re-incarnate in another. The choice is open to him either to live a disembodied existence for all eternity or to remain as a Master of Wisdom for a considerable time, at any rate, on the earth. In the latter case he holds some Office in the occult Hierarchy, and helps in a large variety of ways the development of humanity. Those who attain Liberation (or Adeptship, in Western terminology) yet who remain on earth, are of course not subject to the limitations of ordinary men. They have attained the goal, therefore all the Higher Planes are open to them. Moreover their consciousness is one of perpetual Joy. In whatever work they may be engaged, this joy-consciousness never leaves them. Being Adepts in Yoga they can perform miracles,[2] but seldom choose to do so, because except in very rare circumstances they regard all miracle-working as a form of exhibitionism. Indeed

[1] Nirvana is not annihilation, as uninitiated Orientalists have supposed. On the contrary it is the very opposite; it is one-ness with Life Itself, yet without loss of individuality. The only annihilation involved is that of all limitations, all human weaknesses and selfishness.

[2] The *modus operandi* by which all miracles are performed is to be found in the *Aphorisms of Patanjali*.

their lack of vanity is so complete, that despite their nobility and great powers, they have been modest enough to term themselves the Elder Brothers and Servants of Humanity, since, in their own words, they live to serve as well as to guide, for those who guide do but serve.

Yet in their guidance they never interfere with the workings of free-will, for that is against the Law. They suggest but they never coerce ; they inspire but never command. Their activities, in fact, are so numerous and varied, and have been so eloquently delineated by that great orator and disciple, Dr Annie Besant, that I cannot do better than quote from her pamphlet on *The Masters* :

They aid, in countless ways, the progress of humanity. From the highest sphere They shed down light and life on all the world, that may be taken up and assimilated as freely as the sunshine, by all who are receptive enough to take it in. . . . Next, the Masters specially connected with religions use these religions as reservoirs into which They pour spiritual energy, to be distributed to the faithful in each religion through the duly appointed " means of grace". Next comes the great intellectual work, wherein the Masters send out thought-forms of high intellectual power to be caught up by men of genius, assimilated by them and given out to the world ; on this level also They send out Their wishes to Their disciples, notifying them of the tasks to which they should set their hands. Then comes the work in the lower mental world, the generation of the thought-forms which influence the concrete mind and guide it along useful lines of activity in this world, and the teaching of those who are living in the heavenly world. Then the large activities of the intermediate world, the helping of the so-called dead, the general direction and supervision of the teaching of the younger pupils and the sending of aid in numberless cases of need. In the physical world the watching of the tendencies of events, the correction and neutralizing, as far as law permits, of evil currents, the constant balancing of the forces that work for and against evolution, the strengthening of the good, the weakening of the evil.[1]

It will be seen from this that although the Masters may have their heads in Heaven, their feet walk the earth, which is another way of saying that they are no vague dreamers but eminently practical men. They have shed all the vices and weaknesses of ordinary mortals, it is true, but they have plodded through those vices and weaknesses themselves on the way towards Adeptship. Therefore their attitude is one of complete understanding and tolerance, combined

[1] The recent benefic aspect of Jupiter to Uranus, early in July 1932, was thus utilised by them to bring the Lausanne Conference to an unexpectedly successful issue after the preliminary discussions had threatened to prove abortive.

with a great sympathy and what is equally important, as they say themselves—a pronounced sense of humour. This latter, among their many other qualities, was engagingly apparent when that remarkable woman and initiate, H. P. Blavatsky, towards the end of last century founded the Theosophical Society, and first brought the Masters Koot Hoomi and Morya to the notice of an unreceptive world. Since that time, however, a certain element of sacerdotalism has crept into the Society, and the Masters have come to be looked upon rather as glorified parsons : a distinction to which they prefer not to lay claim. It is always difficult to dissociate any form of ecclesiasticism from sectarian points of view, and as one of the great ideals which the Masters seek to inculcate is Unity in Diversity, this attitude is to be deprecated. And even more to be deprecated is the policy to which Alice Bailey draws attention in her admirable book, *Initiations Human and Solar*. She writes :

Certain schools of occultism and of theosophical endeavour have claimed to be the sole repository of Their teaching, and the sole outlet for Their efforts, thereby limiting that which

They do, and formulating premises which time and circumstance will fail to substantiate. They work most assuredly through such groups of thinkers, and throw much of Their force into the work of such organizations, yet, nevertheless, They have Their disciples and Their followers everywhere, and work through many bodies and many aspects of teaching. Throughout the world, these Masters have come into incarnation at this time with the sole intent of participating in the activities and occupations and truth-dissemination of the various churches, sciences and philosophies, and thus producing within the organization itself an expansion, a widening, and a disintegration where necessary, which might otherwise be impossible. It might be wise for occult students everywhere to recognize these facts, and to cultivate the ability to recognize the hierarchical vibration as it demonstrates through the medium of disciples in the most unlikely places and groups.

Nevertheless even if some members of the Theosophical Society have been inclined to fall into the sectarian error mentioned of arrogating to the Society the sole right to receive and give forth the Masters' teachings, let us not forget how much we are indebted to that Society and its leaders for the wealth of occult knowledge which it has offered to the world. It is merely regrettable that the vast output of Theosophical literature does not circulate as freely as could be desired.

PERFECT CO-OPERATION BETWEEN THE MASTERS

The ideal of Unity in Diversity to which I have referred, is so completely realized by the Masters that although on the surface they may sometimes appear to be working in opposition, in reality they are working in perfect accord, their manifold branches of activity blending with one another as do the colours of the spectrum.

Thus last century when Victorian bigotry and religious narrow-mindedness had reached a climax, one of the Masters, in order to counteract this, inspired the Agnostic Movement. This in its turn showed signs of becoming over-emphasized, so to adjust the balance another of the Masters inspired the Spiritualistic Movement. A little later Master Koot Hoomi and Master Morya sponsored the Theosophical Society through their much-maligned disciple, Madame Blavatsky. Then yet another Master inspired Christian Science. All these Movements were operative simultaneously, and each in opposition to the other. Haeckel swept aside belief in the soul as pure superstition, Madame Blavatsky informed the spiritualists that their spirits were but empty shells, while

Mrs Eddy pronounced Theosophy to be an "error of mortal mind", and Victorian bigots condemned each and all of these Movements as anti-christian machinations of the devil. Meanwhile the Masters, although they deplored these intolerant denunciations, patiently watched each Movement to gauge its effect on the great Evolutionary Scheme, towards the carrying out of which they work so harmoniously together.

MASTERS AND PUPILS

It will be inferred from what has been previously said that the Masters take pupils, but it is essential to state unequivocally that any successful attempt to set up a rapport with these Super-men entails a life of self-abnegation and rigorous self-discipline. The indulgence in cocktail drinking and immoderate sexuality, to which many people are addicted at the present time, is entirely hostile to Occult Science: the former poisons the organism, the latter wastes force. Again, people whose minds are sullied by jealousies and spites and other forms of uncharitableness cannot hope to become receptive to the finer vibrations until drastic steps have been taken to overcome these weaknesses. It may be objected that many cases are extant where the possession of psychic faculties is coincident with imperfections of character. True, but such faculties are seldom reliable and are usually of the lower type known as astral psychism.[1] As a rule they are faculties brought over from a past incarnation, in which some form of Yoga or some kind of magic has been practised. Unfortunately a large number of such psychics have " rushed into print " and made asseverations claimed to be based on some high authority who is nothing but a figment of their own imagination or some spook masquerading as a sage. Scores of such books have been published within the last thirty years, the result being a mass of confusion, baffling to the sincere seeker, and bringing occultism into bad repute. Rightly did that great exponent of Vedanta Philosophy, Swâmi Vivekanânda, say to his pupils : " Reject everything that does not appeal to your reason, no matter who says it."

[1] Such as crystal-gazing, fortune-telling and other clap-trap manifestations.

And now to give a few biographical details regarding him who elects to write under the pseudonym of David Anrias, thus retaining the name under which he figured in my recent book, *The Initiate in the Dark Cycle*.

Coming from a Celtic stock, already as a child he was of a distinctly meditative disposition and much prone to solitary wanderings and day-dreaming. In early manhood, between 1908-14 he came into contact with books on occult science and particularly on astrology which aroused his keen interest and prompted him to make a serious study of the subject. Previous to this he had had an artistic training, and showed remarkable aptitude for pencil portraiture.

Then the war came. Two years he spent in the the trenches and was awarded the Military Medal for running messages under fire. Later on he received a commission in the field and was transferred to the Flying Corps. After the termination of hostilities, he felt a strong inner urge to go out to India, where he worked under Dr Annie Besant, of whom he speaks with great admiration. During that time

he spent many months together in the Nilgiri Hills,
and it was there that with untiring patience, self-
sacrifice and perseverance he applied himself to that
laborious process of " stilling the modifications of the
mind ", to which I have previously alluded. After
years of effort he succeeded in establishing a rapport
with the Adept known as the Rishi of the Nilgiri
Hills, to whom he acquired the capacity of mentally
" tuning in ".[1] This venerable Sage specializes in
Astrology, and it is to his tuition that Anrias owes
his really remarkable proficiency in that most difficult
and misunderstood science. He it was who urged
him to publish some astrological prognostications in
The Theosophist, which, although they provoked a
certain scepticism at the time, have since been fulfilled.

Towards the end of the seven years which Anrias
spent in India, he finally acquired the power to " tune
in " to several of the other Masters of Wisdom, to
which fact we are indebted for the utterances and
portraits contained in this book.

Anrias returned to England in 1927 in order to
make a study of the psychic conditions over here,

[1] See *The Initiate in the Dark Cycle*, Chapter VII.

and to perform certain work in conjunction with other pupils of the Adepts. This book is one such piece of work, for I should point out all that discoveries or pronouncements on the part of one individual should permit of verification by others ; or, more colloquially expressed, in order to arrive at the truth, the " findings " of one man should be " checked up " by others capable of so doing. This rule applies in material Science, it also applies in Occult Science. That none of the pronouncements from the Masters published in this book have suffered through faulty transmission has been verified by the other pupils mentioned previously.

THE PORTRAITS AND THE TEXT

Finally we come to the reason why some of the Masters have permitted their portraits to be given to the world, a matter which will be of special interest to Theosophists.

Within the last year or two Mr Krishnamurti, now of world-wide reputation, has been preaching a form of philosophy in which he has depreciated the

value of the Masters as Teachers and Guides.[1]   The
result is that many erstwhile devotees are no longer
such, and have, as they imagine, embraced Mr Krishnamurti's philosophy while all the time they have
not been in a position to comprehend it.   Although
Mr Krishnamurti himself is fully persuaded that he
has attained Liberation and consequently unconditional Joy, many of his devotees show all too clearly
by their mien and other *insignia* that they have
failed to follow his example.   In fact they were much
more at peace when they believed in the Masters than
they are now ; for a miscomprehension of a philosophy
is almost worse than no philosophy at all.

In view of this, and other considerations too
elaborate to be dealt with here, the Masters mentally
impressed their portraits on David Anrias for re-
production in this book, so that they may serve as
a focus for meditation on the part of those who are
struggling in the waters of spiritual uncertainty, and
for others as well.

I as the writer of this introduction who have
enjoyed the great felicity of contact with three or

[1] This matter has been fully dealt with in *The Initiate in the Dark Cycle*.

four of the Masters, appreciate to the full their value as an ideal to be aspired towards by the serious-minded. Yet how is this aspiration possible unless they provide us with some convincing indication that they exist as realities ? Hitherto the Theosophical Society has jealously guarded such few portraits of them as it possessed ; and although this policy is excusable because actuated by motives of reverence, the Masters themselves now wish it to be discontinued : hence this book. But even so there are certain re-servations. Unlike parsons who, in accordance with custom, draw attention to their calling by " the cut of their cloth", the Masters endeavour on the contrary to deflect all attention from themselves on the physical plane, so that no one shall obtain an inkling as to their true identity. They even have recourse on occasions to adopting some trifling characteristic which almost looks like a fault—a fact which reminds us, by the way, that in order to be perfect, it is sometimes necessary to appear *im*perfect. For instance, in my book, *The Initiate in the Dark Cycle*, one of the English Masters is correctly portrayed as talking in short clipped sentences, a matter which has aroused criticism.   But as he has since explained, he deliberately adopted that particular mannerism because it is the custom to talk like that in the rural district which he inhabits, and in which he desires to remain inconspicuous.   Were he to let it be known that he is a High Initiate, inroads on his valuable time, selflessly used in the service of humanity, be it remembered, would prevent him from pursuing his work.   Therefore only those Masters who live in the to us inaccessible fastnesses of Thibet or other secluded regions have permitted their portraits to appear.   Masters who move in the world of men, such as those portrayed in *The Initiate in the New World* and *The Initiate in the Dark Cycle*, have been obliged to withhold theirs, lest they be recognized. Master Hilarion, however, has made a compromise by giving one portrait of himself functioning as an Arhat in a previous incarnation as St. Paul.   Also I should mention that the portrait of the Master Serapis conveys an impression of him taking a Devic form.[1]

---

[1] It should likewise be conveyed that those of the Mahachohan and the Venetian Master are as they appear to certain Western students in their meditations.

With regard to the language in which the Meditations are clothed, it is largely that of the transmitter, though often flavoured by turns of phrase characteristic of the individual Master concerned. To those who have never studied Occultism, the notion of planes on which thoughts can be expressed and transmitted without the clumsy medium of words may appear baffling and incomprehensible. And yet such planes undoubtedly exist, as may be inferred by the asseverations of many mystics throughout all ages, who have declared that it is well-nigh impossible to *describe* their experiences. Even in every-day life we know that words often distort ideas rather than convey them accurately to the mind of another. It is therefore to be looked upon as an advantage rather than otherwise that faculties may be developed by means of which thoughts can be flashed in an instant of time from one mind to another without the retarding vesture of words. And it is in this manner that the Masters communicate through space one with another, and also with those of their pupils who are advanced enough to respond to their particular vibrations.

In conclusion I may point out that although only nine of the Masters feature in this book, there are about sixty at the present time who are incarnate in bodies of various nationalities. In addition to the other powers they possess, they have that of retaining their physical body far beyond the usual span of three score years and ten, and moreover of prolonging its efficiency, and even its appearance of comparative youthfulness, in some cases for several hundred years.

Yet it is not for this prolongation of youthfulness —which is merely incidental—that they seek to guide others to the Path, but because they wish that others should participate in that greater Power, greater Utility and unconditional Joy which they experience themselves.

I

THE RISHI[1] OF THE NILGIRI HILLS

Imagine the great heavenly bodies, stars and planets alike, ensouled by living Beings of inconceivable force and majesty and beauty.

Imagine, emanating from each of these living centres, vital currents which thrill through space.

Imagine these currents, which represent the life-essence of each of these mysterious stellar and planetary existences, radiating from them as mighty waves of colour, waves of sound, which although beyond the power of human sense to apprehend, nevertheless influence every particle and atom which they contact, every psychic and spiritual factor of Man's being.

The law of the Universe being absolute Unity, not one single emanation from the most far-off star-being but what must affect, to a greater or lesser degree, his brothers in space.

[1] Sage.

The mystery of Life is indeed hidden in the stars, and it is for the true astrologer to decipher and interpret it to his fellows.

To certain Masters whose line of evolution in the past has enabled Them to sense and see the cosmic life-currents as realities, falls the task of adapting them to the needs of this particular planet. Like outposts they stand to guard it from the impact of powers so tremendous that they prove destructive and disintegrating unless transmuted before coming into contact with the earth. This applies to the forces emanating from Uranus and Neptune, while the gentler currents of Jupiter, Saturn, Mercury and Venus, in the charge of Adepts who have evolved along those particular lines, are allowed full scope.

But occasionally for the evolution of humanity, the vibrations of the outside planets are permitted to play upon the earth. This inevitably brings in its train upheavals, wars and crises of all descriptions, for it is the especial function of the aforesaid planets to destroy for the sake of building anew. The recent inrush of Neptunian and Uranian forces, seen by us as great waves of indigo and rapid shafts of white light alternating with other colours, were responsible for the world war[1], in itself but a reflection of the turmoil on the inner planes, which is to lead to ultimate regeneration, and has involved the taking of higher initiations by even such mighty Beings as the Planetary and Solar Logoi.

This occult and physical upheaval will in course of time involve a change in the whole race. Among other things, certain *chakrams* or centres in the etheric body will need to be developed in an order different from what has hitherto been found essential by Him who is the Manu[2] of the Fifth Root Race. We who

---

[1] Note for astrological students. The cause of this upheaval was the Lunation of January 11th, 1910, when the opposition of Uranus to Neptune was in evil aspect to the exoteric planets Saturn, Jupiter and Mars. With the benefics Venus and Mercury rendered powerless, there was nothing to stop the combination of Uranian destruction and Neptunian disintegration from demonstrating the full malefic effect of the opposition aspect, and acting as exoteric influences upon the earth.

Needless to say, if humanity had so far transcended the vices and passions which lead to war, these aspects would not have had to work in this particular way, but would have manifested in some less physically destructive fashion, or even taken the form of some great mental stimulus.

But as it was, many egos took the opportunity of the war to wipe off past Karma and purify their higher vehicles through the sacrifice entailed.

[2] When Vaivasvata, the Manu or Ruler, founded the Fifth Root Race, he reversed the order in the occult development of the etheric centres in the body. This he did partly to counteract Black Magic, prevailing at the time, and partly to separate off his new sub-race from the old and enable them to respond to higher vibrations. Similarly several centuries in advance, he will make a change in the etheric centres in that sub-race from which the new

specialize in the study of this type of work as well as in the direction of the cosmic currents, are ever hoping, searching for possible pupils, sufficiently sensitive, yet able to approach these problems in what your Western World calls the scientific spirit.

Even before the war, you, my son, through your astrological studies, were learning to become responsive to the vibrations of the outside planets.

It was I who caused you to be led to India and to live for several years within the aura of my *ashrama*[1] in the Nilgiri Hills. Here you were gradually prepared for the work of helping us to focus the higher forces of Uranus and Neptune upon those who will ultimately learn to express them both as Power and Love, as breadth of mental vision and spiritual intuition.

During this period of transition, when the outcome of chaos has not yet resolved itself into harmony, those chelas on the second or Love Ray feel most of

---

Sixth Root Race is to spring ; this is in order to assist the next Manu in his future work. This change is even now taking place in the United States of America, the horoscope of which contains powerful planetary influences in the three airy signs, Libra, Aquarius and Gemini. The last sign contains the occult key to a development which must remain esoteric for some time. See *Adepts of the Five Elements* by David Anrias (Routledge).

[1] Occult centre and home.

all the lack of love around them. Many have felt it so much that they have withered and died for want of the great nourishing force which has hitherto sustained them.

Others like Krishnamurti, who have been inspired by Devas associated with the new planetary forces to assume the *rôle* of Shiva, the Destroyer, have lost touch with their original ray in their attempt to live and live positively in this grim cycle. You who were able to predict his future development can realize the difficulties which beset him.

Cosmic Aquarian forces, impersonal as the wind itself, playing upon his consciousness, impelled him ceaselessly to express that which he had acquired with so much difficulty—the Aquarian ability to become liberated from all need of human and super-human associations. This ability in itself is only an exercise in meditation, and no more than an aid to the ideal of attaining union with God through the entire subjugation of personal desire. Many exponents of this school of philosophy, however, instead of becoming "liberated", will find themselves so placed when they reincarnate that they will be

forced to learn, first the lessons of physical plane
co-operation, and then self-conscious control of the
astral body.

For the astral body can neither be ignored nor
dispensed with. On the contrary it is frequently
the only means through which the majority of the
Fifth Race and the whole of the Fourth Race can
learn their lessons and train the will. Similarly a
repressed astral body is no acquisition and leads
nowhither. Your modern Western psychology, our
gift to the world through inspired sources, has proved
this. But what the West has yet to evolve is the
desire to control the emotional body. When this desire
becomes sufficiently powerful, a form of Yoga will be
given and tested through a group of pupils, to become
general knowledge only when the time is ripe.

Those noble souls who are capable of controlling
and transmuting every desire, every emotion in order
to attain some great ideal, respond to the higher
vibrations of Mars. The whole sympathetic system,
in their case, is polarized to that centre within the
heart which answers to the call of Service. The astral
body is raised to the Buddhic plane through the

transmuting fire of selfless action.* Great soldiers and organizers frequently take this line, and through their self-sacrifice become pupils of my Brother Morya. Meditate upon him if you would comprehend something of the lofty aims which he is ever seeking to inspire in the leading minds of to-day.

* The Master Morya has decided during the last fourteen years, that the world in general is destined to evolve through the study and then the control of the subconscious mind. Hence some sort of training must be evolved to enable people to accomplish this.

To those who have already "arrived" this training is not essential. He, as potential Manu of the Coming Race, is now making a study of the race subconscious, particularly that aspect which relates to the desire for domination over others. This desire has menaced every civilization and is largely responsible for conflicts in personal, national and international relationships. By using his Arhat form, and projecting it into the race subconscious, through the element air and the planet Uranus, he is helping those responsive to the Aquarian vibration to rise above personal desires, and achieve victory over the self.

This procedure is admirably expressed by Him in *Agni Yoga:*

"The subtle body of the Yogi, liberated, visits different planes of existence. Flights into space and plunges into the *depths* of the planet are equally attainable. . . . Such realization is needed to the progress of the spirit. Such striving towards perfection will come through the realization of *imperfection*."

II

MASTER MORYA

I will say but little, being one who is expressed through action rather than words.

The basic truths of the inner life, service, co-operation and mutual tolerance, will become the bed-rock of the future civilization, and towards that end I work and serve humanity. Passing phases of self-indulgent introspection, apparent everywhere in the highly-civilized cities of the West, are for intellectual *poseurs* perhaps, who are not as yet ready for occultism, but hardly for those who have once put their feet upon the Path.

For these last there can be no looking back nor dallying by the way.

A goal was needed at the end of the last century, submerged in doubt or superstition, and that goal for the coming race has been both finely expressed and lived in the outer world by my leading disciple, Annie Besant, for over forty years.

MASTER MORYA

A Rajput Prince. Occupied Akbar's body in a previous incarnation.
Resides at Shigatse

Previous to that, the scheme of evolution, covering vast cycles of time was described by that great initiate, Helena Petrovna Blavatsky, in her monumental work the *Secret Doctrine*—an achievement which will live for centuries to come, long after the smaller sub-cycles with their special problems are over and forgotten. With these I am not concerned. If you could become one with my consciousness, you would find it concentrated only upon service and action, born of a continuous urge to help mankind. You may consider this " functioning collectively ", and think that influencing men through crowd psychology based upon broad concepts has serious disadvantages ; nevertheless the large-hearted will answer to the call. If they fail now is no matter, they will succeed in the next life, and towards such as these my love goes forth always. Repressions and smaller vices they may have ; yet I love them all, and however dark the times may be, even in the greatest darkness and doubt, there am I always with them, though unseen by mortal eyes.

My great disciple H. P. Blavatsky, who founded the Theosophical Society, and who suffered ceaselessly that it might live, is even now about to return to the world that calls for help on every side. She has but to select her medium of return and *master it*, and she will be with you on the physical plane. Through her I shall once more become expressed, even in this dark cycle, despite the evil forces which absorb into themselves and utilize all the destructive elements around.*

* Although this was the Master's plan, its fulfilment was dependent on H. P. Blavatsky's voluntary acceptance of it. The second world war within the Cycle of Mars was approaching. As the time was short within the cycle, it would seem that she preferred to return to the world, for a longer period, and in more auspicious circumstances.

H. P. Blavatsky had 28° Cancer rising, the Solar number, and thereby became attuned to the universal etheric element latent in the Pisces decanate of Cancer and appertaining to the passing Age. Her mind became absorbed in superconscious phenomena and she was able to project it backward or forward through a psychological identification with the superconscious Solar element in nature. In her next life, like everyone else, she will be subject to the peculiar limitations of the Libra decanate of the Aquarian Age; for the occult powers of the passing Age are *rapidly becoming short-circuited*. A close conjunction between the Sun and Neptune in Virgo might be used to achieve this subtle apotheosis in connection with the race-subconscious.

(Neptune was in Virgo between 1928 and 1943.)

From *Man and the Zodiac*, page 111.

MASTER ROOT HOOMI LAL SINGH

Of Kashmiri origin; studied at Oxford in 1950. Pythagoras in one of his previous incarnations. Resides at Shigatse

MASTER KOOT HOOMI LAL SINGH

Of Kashmiri origin. Studied at Oxford in 1850. Pythagoras in one
of his previous incarnations. Resides at Shigatse

III

MASTER KOOT HOOMI

When you were here in India, my son, and wrote upon the necessity of establishing an international outlook, you never imagined that a crisis in the world's finance would so soon create a situation which would bring this pressing necessity nearer to the minds of men.[1] In these days when finance has become so international that a panic in Wall Street immediately reacts upon the Bourse and the Stock Exchange, it would seem to be obvious that modern Western civilization can no longer be run on the principles of the jungle. Unfortunately this has not yet been realized by your leading financiers and administrators, who are nevertheless suddenly called upon to remedy previous errors, largely the inheritance of their predecessors, without the necessary spiritual wisdom and self-discipline which this terrible situation demands.

It is not too much to say that we of the White Lodge anticipated such a situation, and endeavoured,

[1] See *The Initiate in the Dark Cycle*, Chapter X.

as far as lay in our power, to mitigate it in advance by stressing the necessity for Brotherhood and Co-operation if civilization was to survive. Christianity having been proved inaccurate according to the scientists and historians of the last century, drastic means had to be adopted to counteract complete materialism. We tried to startle people by H. P. Blavatsky's etheric phenomena, and when that method failed, we attempted at least to arrest their attention and to prove our own existence by means of her psychic powers. It was hoped that the *Secret Doctrine*, her life-work, would make men pause to think, or at least speculate, if only a little, upon its vast range of occult lore.

Within the time permitted by the Lords of Karma for the inauguration of a new spiritual movement, we did all that was possible to avert the impending world-crisis. That much of the effort missed its object was partly because the details of the great scheme had perforce to be worked out by pupils, still subject to their own Karmic limitations, and partly also because humanity at large was not yet capable of receiving what we had to give.

As regards the immediate difficulties of the Theosophical Society itself, action and reaction being equal and opposite, it was inevitable that its previous period of intense outer activity, propaganda and blind obedience to established occult authorities, should be succeeded by a period of doubt and questioning of all authority. Some members of the Society saw themselves as sheep stampeded first down one path and then another, after a brief phase of indecision, when there suddenly appeared to be several shepherds each of whom openly disagreed with the other as to which path to take. Whereas formerly the recognized shepherds were trusted and eagerly obeyed, at present confusion reigns, and there would seem to be no shepherd at all.

For a time the Society will be given over to a period of introspection and self-searching, the result of Krishnamurti's teaching. But as no teacher has the sole monopoly of wisdom, he must inevitably be succeeded by another whose *dharma*[1] it is to express it from a different angle. Some original thinker will arise, magnetic enough to draw around him a group

---

[1] Work or duty for one particular incarnation.

of pupils who will share his views and aspirations. It
is for us to see that the right personality appears at
the auspicious moment, and not before. This is one
of our most difficult tasks—to know when a cycle is
ending and another beginning.

Contraction must always follow expansion, in the
occult world as in the material. As you know, at the
end of each century there is a great outpouring of
spiritual force from the Lodge. This must of necessity
slowly die down, to make way for the new outpouring
and its expression in a new form. Krishnamurti's
teachings worked in harmony with the law of cycles
in causing a contraction after a period of expansion
which had already exhausted the force from the initial
impulse of the last century.

Any great initiate who comes in the near future
will only have the force of his own egoic group to draw
upon, and will need to be a powerful personality indeed,
if he is to contend with the spiritual vacuum which is
gradually making itself everywhere perceptible. Only
the bravest of souls dare attempt what will inevitably
become a struggle to keep the lamp of truth alight until
the fresh flowering of faith at the end of the century.

We who watch the struggles of humanity with compassion, with understanding, who applaud their victories and sympathize with their failures, realize the suffering with which the present phase is fraught, the heart-break which it has entailed for many. Yet we would not put an end to it, even if it lay in our power. Where you see merely the wastage of frustrated effort, uncertainty, chaos, petty jealousies and bewilderments—the broken fragments of an as yet uncompleted pattern, in fact—we see that pattern a little more in perspective, each fragment an integral factor in the perfection of the whole. We know that the suffering may be likened to spiritual growing-pains ; we know the spiritual strength and self-reliance, the joy, the illumination and the expansion which for each individual may be the outcome of the present agony.

After the period of spiritual darkness, I foresee a period of what may be termed spiritual aridity.

During the coming fifty years the intellectual mind will tend to become isolated and entirely immersed in its own problems. Not only art and music, but even such concepts as Spiritualism, will be practically reduced to the level of scientific formulae.

Then gradually at first, subtly as a thread of melody weaving itself in and out of harsh dissonances, a gentler element will come to supersede the foregoing crudity and dryness, a greater reaching out towards that Beauty and Mystery which are veritably as the garments of God.   Art and music[1] will be more direct in their appeal to the heart and spirit of Man ; the eternal quest of the Mystic will again be stimulated by fresh outpourings of Wisdom and Love from the Higher Planes.

Therefore, though I feel for what many of my followers are going through in this Cycle of Darkness,[**] I can look with serenity upon their tribulations, knowing that towards the end of the century they shall once again be gathered round me to help forward the work begun in this life, but so often crowned not with the laurels of success, but with the thorns of frustration.   Opportunity shall be afforded them to remedy past error, to turn failure into attainment.   They shall find in the outside world a greater receptivity to the message to which at present so many turn a deaf ear.

[1] See *Music, its Secret Influence throughout the Ages* by Cyril Scott (Rider).
[**] See Appendix.

For this time the great influx of power to be poured forth at the end of the century will not fail in its object ; it will be a mighty tide bearing Mankind towards a greater comprehension, greater enlightenment, towards the ineffable blessings of that Peace which passeth all understanding.

As has already been foreshadowed elsewhere,[1] there shall come one, a dearly beloved disciple and messenger of mine and of my brother Jesus, who shall manifest such powers as only those who love and are one with Love have, through the purification of suffering, gained the right to claim . . . One who shall bring joy to the sorrowful, strength to the weak, light to the blind, hope to those who sit in the house of weeping . . . One who shall heal the afflicted and open the ears of the deaf to the secret melodies of the divine spheres . . . One whose consciousness will be pervaded by the Love and Knowledge of God, and gifted with the power to lead others unto that same Joy.

[1] See *The Initiate in the Dark Cycle*, Chapter XV.

IV

MASTER JESUS

Let us continue the theme of my brother Koot Hoomi with the thought that his pupil was also mine in the last life, and will be again in the next. As before she combined teaching with the art of healing, so again, whether she comes this time in a male or female body, she will attempt to synthesize these powers and adapt them to the needs of another generation.

Despite the manifold discoveries of modern medical science, many of the diseases which afflict mankind appear to be growing ever more recondite, less susceptible to treatment by the accepted methods. This is due to the fact that many egos in the effort to become free to tread the path have undertaken to absorb and transmute undesirable elementals or thought-forms created by themselves in past lives, and which in the present life return to attack them in one or other of their subtler bodies before manifesting as strange and

MASTER JESUS

Previous incarnation Joshua, son of Nun ; also Jesus of Nazareth, who was overshadowed by the Christ. Now in a Syrian body. Lives in the Holy Land

baffling ailments in the physical. When the hour of their deliverance is at hand these brave souls will be brought into contact with healers and physicians able to counteract their maladies with the appropriate treatment. Clairvoyant sight will of course be indispensable to determine the origin of the trouble ; and the vibrations of colour and sound will be increasingly utilized to produce healing effects, and to re-build and strengthen not only the higher bodies but the physical itself.

The battle within Man's consciousness shifts its field with every age. Where before the problem was to raise the emotional to the spiritual by means of prayer and aspiration, now it tends to become the effort to conquer desire through analysis. This being so, we who directed the old line of spiritual endeavour must modify to some extent our original methods in order to co-operate with those Adepts and their disciples who are to become associated with the new.

This is not easy to accomplish, and requires the utmost skill in manipulating those guiding and spiritualizing currents which, like electricity, run through the consciousness of Mankind.

The actual transference from one line to the other will cover centuries ; for thousands of souls who are not of a self-analytical type will still be in need of that healing power which prayer alone can give : for it keys, or rather should key, the whole body to one note and thereby enables spiritual aspiration to dominate both mind and desire alike. Also the physical etheric centres become, by the very act of kneeling— itself of great occult significance—attuned to certain currents encircling the earth and ever available to those who desire help from the unseen. By associating prayer with kneeling, man is not only aided, but to a certain extent guarded from pernicious influences liable to dominate him in any other position that the body can assume.

In the Middle Ages, the average man's mental body being but elementary, it readily became quiescent at times of prayer, and the emotions were thus free to receive spiritual illumination. Likewise by gathering together to pray, added power was generated, enabling a group to experience that expansion of consciousness which individuals, praying alone, frequently fail to achieve.

Great expansion of consciousness is generated not only by collective prayer, but also by collective sacrifice such as that entailed by war.

Patriotism is a high ideal which has been grossly taken advantage of by powerful and unscrupulous men, manipulated by the dark forces.* The result is that the psychic currents inspiring patriotic emotion have become tainted.

Those adepts who have hitherto endeavoured to raise mankind to supreme acts of self-abnegation, have had the pain of seeing the fruits of their efforts destroyed, and thousands of thinking survivors of the last war plunged into misery and doubt, feeling that their sacrifice has been in vain.

It is not too much to say that in consequence of this aftermath, those who are on the sixth ray of devotion to an ideal, are seriously handicapped, as the life-currents that sustain them will be polluted for a considerable time.

Because these eager souls are guided by feeling rathei than thought, they become easy victims for the unscrupulous. Therefore added power is being given to men of discriminating intellect such as Norman

* See Appendix.

Angell, who consider patriotism not only futile but actually wicked if it can be manipulated by financiers and politicians for their own ends. This type of mind is rapidly on the increase and impressing public opinion with the urgent need for universal disarmament. And rightly so, as the old expansion of consciousness achieved through sacrifice in battle, is now far outweighed by the devastating effects of modern warfare on mind and body alike.

That the methods resorted to for the achievement of the pacifist ideal are along purely materialistic and practical lines rather than those of appeal to the Christian spirit, is regarded by cynics as yet another slur upon Christianity in its impotence to stop War.

But you, my son, and others who in past lives have suffered from the tyranny and the persecution of the recognized exponents of Christianity, and are prone to criticize it for its failures, should bear in mind that it has failed largely because the teachings have become obscured; because misapprehensions have arisen; because Man has not been great enough to rise to the wonderful opportunities afforded him. Nevertheless it is to Christianity that the West owes

everything that may be termed its civilization : the
care of children and of animals ; the consideration for
others ; the first faint beginnings of co-operation and
brotherhood.

Ceremonial, thought by many to be superfluous
and tawdry, is still in reality absolutely indispensable.
But in the coming cycle it will be raised to a higher
level, made more scientific, and will include the co-
operation of different types of Devas who, working
chiefly through Sound, will enhance the magic and the
potency of the actual ritual.

A new religion will be given out, yet it will be but
a facet of the old. There is but one religion, as there
is but One God. Truth Itself is infinitely greater than
can ever be mirrored in all the teachings, the philosophies, the religions of the world. Each of these catch
and reflect, as it were, one beam of the Light. Whether
the reflection is a true one or not, depends upon the
purity of the mirror.

But upon those souls who, albeit mistakenly,
perhaps, struggle and suffer for the sake of Truth as
they see it, rests ever the blessing of those who
would turn every pain and every sorrow and every

disappointment into glory, into strength, into future beatitude.

. . . . . .

Racial development can no more be hurried than can that of a tree ; so the changes will be gradual as ever from one dispensation to the next. The sixth ray devotional types whose era has dominated the world for two thousand years will by degrees be super- seded by more purely mental ones who will inspire the prevailing thought of the future. This transfer of force to the fifth or mental ray will be achieved by my brother Hilarion who, amongst other activities, is guiding the Spiritualistic Movement.[1] We will co-operate to help Christians to combine the old devotional aspiration with the new desire for scientific proof of survival after death.

[1] See *An Outline of Modern Occultism* by Cyril Scott (Routledge).

V

MASTER HILARION

As my brother Jesus has implied in another connection, man's consciousness shifts its field of activity with every age. The influence of science, manifest in the world of facts, is now beginning to invade the realm of personal emotion. First the thinking minority, and then the remainder of the race will be raised, to use theosophical terminology—from the sixth to the seventh sub-plane of the astral, that region where the world of emotions merges into the world of the mind. This sub-plane is the one on which the average scientist is already functioning; it is also that on which the spiritualist of the future will endeavour to obtain his results.

Although the Spiritualism of to-day is imbued with much that is unsatisfactory, it will become, and is indeed already becoming, a potent factor in the occult education of the race.

Broadly speaking, there are two basic motives which impel people to have recourse to the more exoteric forms of Spiritualism : the desire to lift the curtain which veils the future and the desire to communicate with the dead. The longing to know the future, though springing from a fundamental urge in human nature, is much to be deprecated. Were it possible for it to be revealed to Man what lies hidden upon the path he is destined to tread, he would become far too negative and his spiritual growth would cease. When the future can hold nothing of personal hope or fear, of pain or pleasure, it may be read like the pages of an open book : but that day is far distant from the majority of a race still largely in the thraldom of craving for personal gratification and dread of personal harm. The fact that it is against the occult law, except in very exceptional cases and for very specific reasons, for the Karma of an individual to be shown him in advance, is indirectly and of course quite unconsciously supported and borne out by those professional mediums who, whilst in good faith attempting to satisfy their clients' curiosity, make statements and prognostications which so often prove inaccurate and misleading.

The reason for this inaccuracy in itself lies largely in the fact that the average medium is still exclusively functioning on the sixth sub-plane of the astral, and lacks the ability to discriminate between the various types of entities seeking to impress him, and between what arises in his own sub-conscious mind, or in the minds of his sitters, and what may be *bona fide* messages. Mediums will by degrees come to realize for their own sakes the need of greater emotional control and mental discernment, if their findings are to be reliable and a higher type of spirit is to manifest through them. Similarly, the more cultured the medium and the wider his field of knowledge, the better the results ; for it is but reasonable that the quality of the spirit and of the contact he is able to make, should be dependent upon the quality of the vibration he may find, active or latent, in the medium.

In respect of the second great urge, communication with the dead is justifiable and possible up to a point : but if indulged in too much, it is apt to make those left behind lose their interest in their Karmic duties

on earth. Likewise it frequently delays those who
have passed over in their ascent to the mental plane.
In cases where such actual delay has not been permitted, and a particular spirit has perforce left the
astral for the mental plane, only his decomposing
shell may remain behind, to be invoked by the unseeing
medium and sitters alike. This danger emphasizes
more than ever the need for incessant vigilance on the
part of the medium, for alone in his ability to discriminate between an astral form still ensouled by a
real person and the *shell* of that person, animated,
perhaps, by some undesirable influence, lies the safe-
guard against the possibility of confusion, imposture
and heart-breaking fraud.

Through such vigilance and rigorous self-discipline
mediums will eventually be able to follow the
spirits of the dead from the astral to the mental,
where the possibility of deception is considerably
minimized.

By degrees more intellectual types of people will
be attracted towards Spiritualism, and their investi-
gations, instead of taking the form of probing into the
future or attempting to contact their dead friends,

will be carried on more in the spirit of scientific inquiry.

   •   •   •   •   •   •

Contemporary scientific research tends more and more to revolve round the concept of a unity underlying all things, and the desire to discover the primary source of manifestation. The scientists—even men like Einstein—are standing only on the threshold of those great cosmic revelations towards the understanding of which all those who work upon the fifth ray continually strive. Their love of absolute Truth will inevitably draw them upward to that realm of pure science where they will see and comprehend at last the workings of that great Law of Causation known to those in the East as the Law of Karma. When this Law is understood, it will be accepted even by the ordinary man as an integral part of his being. He will realize that his smallest acts, his thoughts as well as those events which he now believes to be the work of chance or a vague entity who doles out punishments and rewards, are all subject to this Law of Cause and Effect. Then will its working in relation to the Past, the Present and the Future become a recognized

principle and be taken into proper consideration by
all the administrators of public life.

.   .   .   .   .   .

At the present day neither spiritualists nor
scientists realize that they are both overshadowed by
my influence and so being led towards common
conclusions through their common desire to find
Truth. Books will be published upon the conquest
of the Unseen in which eminent scientists and spiritualists will give their opinions side by side. These
will be in apparent conflict, but later on it will be shown
how they can be reconciled. One of my pupils, an
initiate, will incarnate combining a remarkable scientific mind with a mediumistic body ; his work it will be
to co-ordinate both activities and reveal them to be
but facets of one reality.

There are other lines of activity and development
which I am ever trying to stimulate.

Many of those modern novelists who specialise
in the analysis of emotion are under my guidance.
These, by becoming more and more absorbed in mental
rather than emotional problems, will be included with

painters in the general upward urge towards the mental plane.[1]

The work of helping the artistic type will come within the province of my brother the Venetian Master, the guiding influence behind the Art of the West. Meditate upon him if you would realize something of his point of view both with regard to modern art and the art of the future.

[1] See *The Wheel of Rebirth* by H. K. Challoner (Rider).

VI

THE VENETIAN MASTER

Art as you knew it when you were incarnated in Italy, my son, was considered a necessity by the intelligentsia and taken very seriously. Pagan feeling brought over from previous civilizations expressed itself freely through the artists of the period, side by side with the religious element, which was imposed upon the consciousness of the painter by extraneous conditions rather than arising from real spiritual experience. Such religious scenes and emotions as he attempted to convey were usually conventional and stereotyped, although exquisitely painted in the tradition of the period. Even at the present day a certain proportion of painters still concentrate upon the improvement of the technical side of their work rather than upon the search for some deeper significance in the subject they may be portraying.

It is therefore not surprising that a violent reaction to mere superficial beauty should be felt by

THE VENETIAN MASTER
The painter Paul Veronese in one of his previous incarnations

many modernists who go to the opposite extreme and assert that only by the deliberate cult of the ugly can any real sincerity be achieved. Another reason for this deliberate forsaking of many of the accepted canons of art, is to be found in the competitive difficulties which beset the artist of the present day. In an age when the cinematograph is capable of depicting the most exquisite and varied scenes, the interest in dramatic painting and problem pictures is considerably lessened. Similarly portraits are no longer the fashion now that simplicity of effect is emphasized by bare walls.

These things, together with the present economic pressure, combine to make the modern artist discontented and determined to shock the public into some sort of attention. With this end in view, a certain decadent type has imagined that by taking drugs and venturing to the confines of the unseen, he will become more open to the psychic element and gain some unique personal experience enabling him to paint something sensational enough to achieve the desired effect. Occultists, however, who have the gift of vision, can see that the grotesque figures and chaotic patterns which are the result of these strivings and claimed to be *subjective,* are only such thought-forms, usually undesirable, as may be seen upon the lowest sub-planes of the astral. To that extent they are subjective and no more.

Forced back upon himself, the artist will in time come to recognize that his art can in no true sense be furthered by the approach to the problems of the unseen *via* the questionable door of drugs or doubtful magic : in fact that he is merely likely to become a victim of those forces which endeavour to destroy him who attempts to enter the next world without the necessary occult training, which, amongst other things, involves rigorous self-discipline and the cultivation of the faculty of clairvoyance. The artist of the future, better equipped in this respect than his colleague of to-day, will indeed achieve the realization of the higher planes : planes, the beauty of which he will not only be able to contact, but actually to convey to others by means of his painting. Art, once the handmaiden of religion, but in this materialistic age completely divorced from it, will again fulfil its highest function, that of inspiring reverence in the beholder.

It will have worked out its Karmic descent into the abyss, and will once more be on its upward ascent towards the light. My brother Serapis will co-operate with me in training the artistic mind of the future, and specialize in helping to make it more responsive to the influence of the higher types of Devas.

Meditate upon him if you would know something of what is ahead in this new Era, when, perhaps, for the first time in the civilization of the West, the desire for truth as well as for beauty will alike inspire the heart of the artist.

VII

THE MASTER SERAPIS

Each Age covering a period of about two thousand years has its own zodiacal sign, its own planetary force. When a transition takes place from one Age to another and hence from one sign to another, certain Adepts who for centuries may have been preparing for their office by meditation and study, take over the work of inspiring the new cycle.

For nearly two thousand years the earth has been under the watery sign Pisces ruled by Neptune, the main features of which have been the establishing of Christianity and the conquest of the ocean. Now the new cycle has begun, Aquarius, an airy sign, is influencing men's minds along scientific lines in every direction, especially towards the conquest of the air.

Gradually the emotional Neptunian era which has passed through varying phases of religious ecstasy, superstition, confusion and doubt[1] is merging into the Era of Uranus, Lord of the Air, who inaugurated his

[1] As this process of merging covers several centuries, this statement does not conflict with the ideas about Neptune conveyed elsewhere.

MASTER SERAPIS

Greek by birth. Works with the Deva Evolution. Dwelling-place
may not be revealed

rule by striking the note of atheism and the worship of scientific facts, and will culminate it by leading men towards the direct knowledge of God.

Uranus, then, as the ruler of Aquarius, will guide and inspire the future leaders of the race. Original thinkers, inventors, scientists, artists, writers and all those who function as individuals rather than collectively, will, in ever-increasing numbers, come under his sway as the age unfolds.

The greatest Uranian characteristic, perhaps, is the desire for freedom of thought, together with the search for new methods of living and a refusal to accept or be dominated by the outworn or traditional, no matter how beautiful it may have been.

The meaning underlying Aquarius, the sign which has baffled astrologers throughout the ages, is even now very difficult to delineate, so varied are the types of men born under its influence, so petty in some cases, so great in others. The esoteric key to its significance however, and one which has hitherto been kept secret, is to be found in the interpretation of its symbol.[1]

[1]

If this symbol is considered as the usual two horizontal undulating lines, it indicates man fettered to the earth by the customs of the times through those invisible thought-currents which encircle the earth and influence humanity in general. But regarded vertically, it represents that point at which the circle of desire, as expressed through the animal nature of the other zodiacal signs, is left for the spiral, and Aquarius, the man, begins his ascent towards God. Carrying this latter symbol even further, the first downward current is the Ego endeavouring to comprehend and control the personality by analysing his own feelings in order to free himself from fear and superstition and arrive at truth ; and the ascending current represents him who has finished with desire, and has no more to learn on this planet.

In the combination of Uranus and Aquarius we have possibilities of spiritual development so vast and comprehensive as to precipitate a great change in the future of the whole race.

Among other things a new religion will be evolved, uniting the spiritual and the scientific elements. The outstanding minds of the New Age will be daring and experimental, and ready to risk much in order to create new standards whereby the welfare of their contemporaries and successors may be furthered.

It is for such as these I work and wait, for they will be willing to co-operate with the Devas of the mental plane who are my special charge. In order to ensure the necessary rapport between Devas and men, some of the advanced scientists, thinkers and artists of the present day are already taking Devic initiations side by side with those of the Great White Lodge.[1] These men are, so to say, the advance-guard of the new type and under the special supervision of the Mahachohan.

---

[1] These initiations involve the response to the influence of Uranus, Neptune and Pluto. These planets are differentiated from other members of our Solar system by their axial rotation.

"Each planet has two movements, one axial, in which it turns on itself completing the recurrent cycle of day and night, and the other orbital, in which it revolves round the central sun completing the cycle of the year. . . Though these three planets move round the sun from East to West, their axial rotation take place in the contrary direction, from West to East.

This variation of movement may be considered symbolic of the re-orientation of values now taking place the world over. Since every outward form has an inner—or spiritual—reality, so the rediscovery of Uranus, Neptune and Pluto indicates the threshold of a fresh evolutionary cycle in which the human race will respond to vibrations of another dimension." (*Towards Aquarius*, by Vera W. Reid.)

VIII

THE MAHACHOHAN

We whose work it is to gauge correctly and counteract, if necessary, the conflicting forces in Space, must know ahead which of the numerous astrological cycles and sub-cycles—all influencing and interpenetrating each other—is to predominate at a given time, and the approximate length of its duration. Just as a skilful mathematician makes his intricate calculations and retains them all in his memory, so are we in our higher consciousness aware of the essentials of planetary problems covering vast periods of time, and concentrate upon those which are the most pressing at the moment.

Sometimes the inner significance of these cycles is impressed upon certain of our chelas or even mundane astrologers, if such there be, who can interpret the movements of the stars correctly and divine the mysteries they symbolize.

THE MAHACHOHAN

Known as the Lord of Civilization. Chief of the Masters. Resides
in the Himalayas

Shortly before the war a major and minor cycle[1] combined to bring about great upheavals; and as you have already been told by your Guru[2], the vibrations of the outside planets were permitted to play upon the earth and act as destroying and regenerating influences on every plane.

The Theosophical Society, the founding of which represented a minor cycle of occult activity emanating from the White Lodge at the close of the last century, will become increasingly open to the influence of these planets. For Uranus and Neptune were rising in the original horoscope, whilst Jupiter, Venus and Mercury were setting.

Henceforward the Uranian influence will form the object of study and deep meditation for no lesser being than the Manu, as will the Neptunian for the Bodhi-sattva[3] of the future Race. They seek to master these currents with a view to helping their pupils to respond to them in cycles to come.

[1] The Lunation of January 11th, 1910 and the thirty-five years' cycle of Mars, March 21st, 1909. * See Appendix.

[2] See I.

[3] Teacher of the Race.

Not for one single step of the road, apparently so tortuous and steep, is Man left to stumble alone. He is ever overshadowed by the blessing of those who watch, those who guide, those who unceasingly work for his ultimate happiness : and above all is he over-shadowed by the blessing of that Great One, the Teacher and Healer of mankind, whose Love eternally enfolds the world and whose presence upon earth will once again be felt and known by those whose hearts are attuned to Him. [1]

[1] See *The Vision of the Nazarene* by Cyril Scott (Routledge).

THE LORD MAITREYA.

Known to Christians as the Christ; to the Orient as the Bodhi-sattva; to Mohammedans as the Iman Mahdi. Appeared in India as Shri Krishna, in Palestine as Jesus, in Great Britain as St. Patrick, whose etheric body he now holds. Resides in the Himalayas. His office is that of World Teacher. He presides over the destiny of great religions.

THE LORD MAITREYA

Known to Christians as the Christ, to the Orient as the Bodhi-sattva, to Mohammedans as the Iman Madhi. Appeared in India as Shri Krishna, in Palestine as Christ, in Great Britain as St. Patrick, whose etheric body he now holds. Resides in the Himalayas. His office is that of World Teacher. He presides over the destiny of great religions

IX

LORD MAITREYA

Those, my son, who would have had me appear in this age as I appeared in Palestine, have failed even to visualize the possibility that I might be limited by Karma in the choice of my medium. For I who hold the office of World Teacher am only permitted to use a physical body selected by the Lords of Karma, and one which needs must express the characteristics of the *zodiacal sign of the future cycle*, rather than those of the sign through which I manifested two thousand years ago.

As you have already realized, the essential difference between the Age which is passing and the Age which is being born, is that Man is learning to leave the world of the emotions in order to enter the kingdom of the mind. The whole of the Western civilization was tending in that direction before Krishnamurti was officially pronounced to be my future medium. Within the limits of his consciousness, untrained in many respects for the difficult task of a Spiritual Teacher, I endeavoured to set the future course whereby Man might follow me to those still higher regions where intuition is enthroned.

You who have studied the horoscope of Krishnamurti know that he is incapable of compromising with the past ; also that he was reinforced in his seemingly destructive work by those great Devas of the Air, who, under the direction of the Lords of Karma, are helping Man to polarize himself towards spiritual rather than material conquests.

In order to co-operate more completely with the Devas, Krishnamurti took initiations along their line of evolution. The essential nature of these Devas, used as agents of the Great Law, being perforce impersonal and detached, it came by degrees to influence his whole point of view, making him appear unsympathetic and even inhuman. Furthermore, since he had attained these initiations in the causal body by a positive effort of consciousness, it became all but impossible for him to be used any longer as my medium.

Every astrological sign has its limitations, and that of the Aquarian is the tendency to become too introspective and self-sufficient, thereby losing contact with other types of men and their lines of development.

Thus although Krishnamurti was right to emphasize the necessity for independent thought, he was wrong in assuming that everyone else, regardless of past Karma and present limitations, could *instantly* reach that point which he himself had only reached through lives of effort, and by the aid of those Cosmic Forces apportioned to him *solely for his office as Herald of the New Age.*

Since by thus in a sense over-reaching his mark my erstwhile medium has brought confusion and bewilderment to the minds of many, it may be thought that this should not only have been foreseen but prevented by the Higher Ones.

Foreseen by Them it undoubtedly was ; but it was not their province to deflect the workings of the Law. It is never for Them to forestall mistakes, if by such mistakes growth may be furthered, but to turn the outcome, wherever possible, to good.

What may arise from the present wreckage of broken shibboleths, traditions and beliefs, from doubt, chaos and soul-anguish, is a new-found determination on the part of the individual to school himself to acquire those faculties which shall enable him to attain by his own efforts a unique and personal contact with the Masters and with God.

Henceforth I come not solely through groups with recognised officials, through organizations rendering me what is often no more than lip-service in their assumptions of Brotherhood ; I come to each and all who love me, no matter of what race, class or creed. The greatness of their need of me, the strength of their desire to see me, shall be the measure of their power to see me. The peasant in the Swiss mountains ; the scientist in his laboratory ; the artist dreaming of his creations ; the mystic and the psychologist ; the spiritualist and the musician—to these and many others I come if their intuition, their inner vision be true enough to recognize me, if there be in their hearts That which responds to the Love which eternally flows forth to them from mine.

Verily has it been proclaimed throughout the ages that God is Love—Love the very essence of the Absolute ; so that even those things which men look upon as emanating from the Dark Forces are but one aspect of that Love which ever seeks to draw all into fusion with Itself.

Therefore by this Power which I hold, this Power of Almighty Love, seek I to draw the hearts of men into unity with that Good, that Happiness, which is for all men the goal, no matter what name they ascribe to it, no matter under what guise and seeming it appears to them. The ways of search be manifold, but on each of these I am ready to meet my own.

And through these my own will I speak, will I walk amongst men when the hour strikes ; not confined to one recognized medium or vehicle, but wherever the light of aspiration is kindled within a heart, there is my medium, there my vehicle.

The combined notes of these ten Great Ones create a chord of harmonious sound in heaven, yet within the aura of the earth for its helping.

He who has learnt to hear this exquisite music has done so by first listening to the note of his own Master, on the inner planes and during meditation.

Aspire towards Him Whom you feel to be your own Master if you would hear on earth, albeit faintly at first, that note which shall ultimately harmonize your heart with His.

APPENDIX TO THIRD EDITION

THE DARK CYCLE OF MARS

By David Anrias author of *Man and the Zodiac*, etc.

Reprinted from *American Astrology Magazine* Year 1940

TO arrive at a dispassionate analysis of existing conditions, the study of astrological cycles can prove very illuminating. The late Alan Leo made several startling and correct prognostications regarding the 35 year cycle of Mars as far back as 1911. To prove the fulfilment of his correct conclusions regarding this cycle and its *predominating influence* over all other configurations, they are quoted from *Modern Astrology*, October, 1911:—

"In the year 1909 at 6.13 a.m. on the 21st March, a cycle of the planet Mars began which remains in force until 1944.

"In this energizing cycle there are many sub-cycles, beginning with 1910 with Uranus as a sub-influence. . . . Each sub-period begins with the Sun's ingress into Aries, the astronomical New Year.

"In the year 1909 when the Sun entered into Aries at London, the sign Aries was rising with the Sun close to the Ascendant and Mars, the ruling planet, was highest in the heavens, exalted in Capricorn and in conjunction with Uranus. Mars, as ruler of the Ascendant, becomes the ruler of the People and their general conditions for the following 35 years.

"Since this new era, there has been a steady manifestation of unrest, disturbance and strikes throughout the land, and this will continue with modifications and accentuations until 1944, affected by the sub-influences and the other planets as follows:—

	Mars	..	..	1909,	16,	23,	30,	37,	44
	Uranus	..	..	1910,	17,	24,	31,	38,
	Venus	..	..	1911,	18,	25,	32,	39,
Sub-	Mercury	..	..	1912,	19,	26,	33,	40,
influences	Neptune	..	..	1913,	20,	27,	34,	41,
	Saturn	..	..	1914,	21,	28,	35,	42,
	Jupiter	..	..	1915,	22,	29,	36,	43,

INFLUENCES OF VARIOUS PLANETS

"Under Uranus we may expect sudden and unexpected developments, drastic changes, and great attempts towards reformation with revolutionary tendencies and much violence; under Venus, opportunities for conciliation and arbitration (viz. 1918); under Mercury, great commercial developments, inventions, etc.; under Neptune, years of crises and great socialistic tendencies; under Saturn, much sorrow and general misery (1914); under Jupiter, religious reforms.

"The cycle of Mars coincides with war, strife and much violence on earth; taxation is high and the governments of the nations are in difficulties."

The fact that—in the main—the world has been dominated by this cycle of Mars requires no elaboration. But it is of interest to check up the sub-influences at work, taking a few years here and there at random. In 1910, a Uranus year, the late King Edward died, whilst later, during this year, the House of Lords was drastically deprived of much of its power. Both in England and elsewhere, 1913 was conspicuous as a year of socialistic tendencies, heralding the year of Saturn, the planet of fate, which precipitated the World War. In 1915, a Jupiter year, war conditions in France remained stationary. But in 1916, the year of double Mars, a great attempt to advance on the Western Front was made by the Allies, resulting in enormous loss of life for all concerned. The next Uranus year, 1917, witnessed a great development of the Air Force and fighting in the air. In 1918 came "opportunities for conciliation and arbitration," foreseen by Alan Leo. This was followed by the Mercury year of indeterminate discussion, which sowed the seed for further difficulties and misunderstandings.

The chart of the Mars cycle is erected for London. Though the planet's house positions would be different in other countries, yet their mutual aspects to each other would remain much the same. The fact that Mars was in conjunction with Uranus, both afflicting Saturn, and in opposition to Neptune, would tend to precipitate a series of world crises throughout the 35 year cycle.

Certain Adepts were fully aware that this cycle would be an extremely critical period, because the pervasive influence of Mars, the planet of Desire, is assigned to the Solar Plexus. This centre is aptly termed "The Web of Life" by Eastern Occultists. The Mars cycle, they knew, would disintegrate the standards and traditions of the passing Pisces Age without much possibility of inaugurating a new Era of constructive thought. In other words, differences between the nations would tend to become more marked, whilst any possibility of mutual co-operation would appear to diminish throughout the cycle.

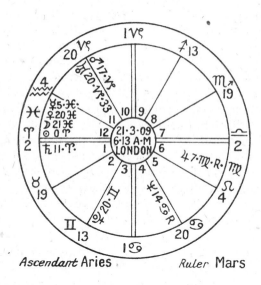

Ascendant Aries   *Ruler* Mars

J. RAMSAY MACDONALD

The same conditions applied to the late J. Ramsay MacDonald, for his chart had similar cross aspects from cardinal signs. His destiny was to be raised to power through the Mars cycle, becoming the first Labour Prime Minister under strenuous and critical circumstances. His endeavour to effect world disarmament at Geneva, during his brief tenure of office, chiefly failed because it was attempted during a bellicose stellar configuration. He should have retired from public life when his progressed Moon transited the cusp of his radical 12th house, the house of secret enemies and frustration, *ruled by Mars and Uranus*. This Lunar progression, afflicting his radical Sun and the 4th house in opposition to Neptune dominating the mid-heaven, caused the involved and baffled condition at the end of his life.

MOST MARKED FEATURE

The most marked feature of the 35 year Cycle of Mars is its afflicted Solar position in the 12th house. This combination enabled disintegrating Uranian-Martian forces, ruling the mid-heaven, to break through and shatter the stable Solar conditions on which our civilization was founded. Because Venus and the Moon and Mercury were in the sign Pisces and in the 12th house, they were short-circuited of emotional expression, hitherto associated with the Pisces Age. Because Jupiter was in the 6th house of health, in opposition to Mercury in the 12th house of introspection and frustration, unsolved mental problems became manifest and forced general attention on the activities of the unconscious mind. Thus psycho-analysis took form as a recognized science of to-day. But Jupiter in the sign of its *detriment* and in opposition to Mercury, proved unfavourable for various attempts to revive certain ceremonial magic of the passing Pisces Age.

Put simply, the forces dominating the world during the present cycle are of the Martian-Uranian type, taking an extreme and startling form of extraversion, calculated to compel the attention of the whole world.

The cycle of Mars has not only had the effect of focussing the interest of the intelligentsia upon the functioning of the unconscious, but it has also influenced the unthinking majority to become easily hypnotized by the positive emotional force of ruthless men. It was a case of "Theirs not to reason why, theirs but to do and die".

HITLER

The Mars conjunction Uranus aspect of the 35 year cycle of Mars forms a benefic trine to Hitler's ruler Venus, in conjunction with his Mars. His *Moon and Jupiter dominate the mid-heaven* of the Martian chart through a powerful conjunction, whilst his Sun is in benefic trine to the Martian mid-heaven also, all involving *earthly* signs and thereby resulting in world recognition. His Saturn is in trine to the other rising Saturn in Aries (Germany's ruling sign), and so he has been able through these powerful, expansive aspects to restore his adopted country's prestige for a period. Nevertheless there is an indication of his over-reaching himself, for his rising planet Uranus* is in exact malefic square to the radical Mars and Uranus of the Martian chart, as well as forming a close affliction with Neptune, the planet ruling the end of this cycle.

In the case of Mussolini, the Mars-Uranus conjunction forms an exact and benefic trine to his radical dynamic Uranus ruling his mid-heaven. Similarly his angular Neptune forms another benefic trine to this conjunction. His Sun and Mercury in Leo form reinforcing trines to the radical Saturn in Aries. His afflictions are more numerous than those of Hitler, and so his success has not been quite so spectacular. His Jupiter and Venus oppose the Mars-Uranus aspect; his Saturn and Moon afflict the radical Jupiter, whilst his Moon and Mars afflict the radical Mercury. These bad aspects indicate numerous frustrations, largely caused by secret enemies. Other difficulties will arise through his afflicted *Moon and Saturn* in conjunction in the 7th house, indicating inefficient or untrustworthy supporters,** who, as Saturn rules his fourth house, may ruin his projects in the end.

* On the downward involutionary arc into matter the cycles of manifestation are 13—the mysterious number mentioned in certain Eastern books. No. 13 is also a Uranus number, 1 + 3 making 4. Hitler knows he responds to this number through Uranus ruling his ascendant. Last year *under Uranus*, he attempted his most spectacular sudden and Uranian actions. On March 13, 1938, Austria became a province of Greater Germany. On September 13, 1938, began the revolt of the Sudetan Germans, which following Hitler's Nuremberg speech, led to the incorporation of the Sudetenland. On March 13, 1939, Hitler sent his ultimatum to Prague. 1939=22=4, also comes under Uranus. So this year under Venus and Uranus still favours Hitler, ruled by those planets.

**Fulfilled at the end of the Mars cycle.

The careers of these remarkable men have only been made possible through the disintegrating forces of the Martian chart, which have reacted unfavourably upon nearly every throne in Europe. Regarding these Martian reactions to the charts of the reigning monarchs of 1910, Alan Leo wrote:

"If a European war breaks out in the lifetime of King George V and the Emperor Franz Joseph, the latter will be the direct cause of drawing England into the struggle."

July Modern Astrology, 1910, p. 294.

"Should England and Germany be engaged in conflict, the horoscope of King George ensures success."

Ibid., p. 293.

"The King of Spain and the Czar of Russia have the same ascendant within a degree; the 8th degree of Virgo, whose symbol is a very strange one. It is a *coach heavily laden with passengers.*"

Ibid., p. 305.

King George VI (then Prince Albert). "Of all the royal horoscopes this is the most marvellous. . . . No less than 7 planets rising. Surely when he comes to the throne King Albert will be a unique king."

Ibid., p. 288.

The King of Italy (yet to be fulfilled). "He will have a tragic end."

Ibid., p. 301.

Although these remarkable men, Hitler and Mussolini, seem to be so powerful, from an astrological point of view they are limited in scope, because the majority of their planets were *setting*. This configuration implies their destiny was to revive national prestige rather than to dominate the world. The careers of both men have largely arisen through their respective nations being hampered by the short-sighted policy of Versailles. As action and reaction are equal and opposite, any Martian policy, *imposed by force*, is just as likely to be ruthlessly shattered. The nations of the world will have to achieve mutual respect and co-operation if civilization is to *survive* and world bankruptcy be avoided at the end of the cycle.

SATURN IN ARIES

Saturn passing through Aries once more, from February 1938 to April 1940, has caused the numerous humiliations, doubts and uncertainties for England (ruled by that sign). This combination of planet and sign has caused her leaders to adopt a hesitating international policy. Let us hope that the passage of Jupiter, the benefic, through Aries from June 1939–May 1940, will restore the national prestige* and enable England's leaders to inaugurate a policy of international co-operation. Saturn in Aries (the sign ruling Germany and England) is an indication of the lack of food, clothing and other necessities for those countries, as well as their heavy taxation. Jupiter's passage through Aries brings temporary political expansion to Germany, largely because Hitler's chart is so amazingly reinforced by that of the Mars cycle.

A TENTH HOUSE SATURN

A German astrologer** informed Hitler some time ago, according to the *Daily Mail*, that "his destiny is to acquire everything he can by peace and that Mars, the planet of war, will be in opposition to him." This advice is based upon the fact that Venus is his ruler rather than Mars and that both afflict Saturn in the mid-heaven, accidentally dignified thereby, but in detriment in the sign Leo. This position of Saturn denotes:

"A precarious condition at some time of the life. Yet the elevation of this planet gives great ambition and desire for public esteem as well as perseverance in attaining the goal If afflicted (as in Hitler's case), there is not sufficient ability to realize individual limitations. There may be a rise, only to fall again through over-estimation of the inherent capabilities. In extreme cases it brings

* Fulfilled by Mr. W. Churchill, his war leaders, and the whole race.
** This man was murdered for saying this.

unusual success followed by dishonour and failure. A fatality hangs over the life at birth."—*Man and the Zodiac*, by the author of this article.

A factor for better conditions in the future is that whereas the horoscopes of Hitler and Mussolini are reinforced by the present Mars cycle, the Lunar cycle of Democracy (1945–80) operates otherwise, for neither of the dictators' charts has affinity with the predominating airy element containing the major planets of the coming cycle. Doubtless Hitler's astrologer has informed him of this fact, hence the dictator's openly expressed realization that his time is short. For his sway over the German race-unconscious is nearly at an end.*

I have already stated, according to Indian Adepts, that the pervasive influence of Mars, the planet of Desire, is assigned to the Solar Plexus. In my book *Man and the Zodiac* I have tried to show how the four central signs are ro-related to that centre also. Thus Leo, patriotic display; Virgo, National commerce; Libra, balance of power; and Scorpio, race domination, alternatively prevail over the race-unconscious.

Men, such as Hitler and Mussolini, with powerful planets *elevated* in these signs of the unconscious, are able to dominate their countrymen thereby, but only so long as the prevailing cycle creates the necessary vortex of force. For this reason the charts of Hitler and Mussolini are given in my book as typical examples of the domination of two magnetic individuals over their expectant but harassed countrymen.

The Uranus trine Neptune aspect, formed at the end of the cycle—from airy or mental signs, augurs an era when international and constructive schemes will be put forward by enlightened men during the Lunar cycle, political proposals such as the world will need if civilization is *to endure*.

* Fulfilled at the end of the Mars cycle.